ONE IS NOT A PAIR

a spotting book

Britta Teckentrup

It's sunny and warm,
and the sky is so blue.
It's time for an ice cream.
I'd like one – would you?

Each cone is the same
as another one there,
but if you look closely
one isn't a pair.

Black-and-white magpies
are building their nests.
They strut and they prance
and they puff out their chests.

Each bird has found something
just like its mate holds,
but one magpie's treasure
is made out of gold.

Here's a squadron of planes,
so fearless and proud.
It's perfect for flying
with barely a cloud.

As they fly round the world
each plane has a pair,
but one does not match
as it zooms through the air.

Here is a farmyard,
where tractors are puffing,
wheels spinning and turning
while engines are huffing.

There's two of each tractor
but there's an exception —
you'll see one is different
with careful perception.

These shiny red cherries
look tasty and sweet,
and some hungry young bees
have stopped for a treat.

The bees are all happily
feasting on lunch,
but which of these fruits
matches no other bunch?

These red-and-white toadstools
are covered in spots,
and the ladybirds too
have splendid black dots.

There are toadstools the same,
with two of each kind,
but there's one with no pair,
which you have to find!

Chirping and cheeping,
birds hop all about
their new wooden houses,
both inside and out.

Each birdhouse and bird
is matched, two by two,
except for one songbird.
I see her; can you?

The birds have now flown
to the tops of the trees
where they witter and twitter
and sing in the breeze.

Each tree has a pair,
where matching birds call,
but one has a guest
that is no bird at all.

On a shelf in the store
are cuddly brown bears,
and each bear has a friend,
for these bears come in pairs.

There's two of each teddy
but one's all alone.
Perhaps he's the one
who most needs a new home.

With bright wooden blocks
you can spend hours and hours,
making new houses
and building tall towers.

Each tower has a pair,
identically laid.
Can you see the one that
is differently made?

They prowl and they preen,
they mew and they purr,
these yowling black cats
with sleek, shiny fur.

One cat's not the same
though he's slinky and thin.
Can you find the cat
that is missing a twin?

When autumn arrives
leaves fall to the ground,
where insects are creeping
and crawling around.

Each leaf and each beetle
is matched by another,
but one of these creatures
is missing his brother.

A packet of pencils
in colours so bright,
are all newly sharpened
to draw or to write.

There's two of each colour,
some red and some green,
but one does not match –
is it one that you've seen?

Stripy and spotty,
and pegged up in rows,
socks dance in a line
as the wind briskly blows.

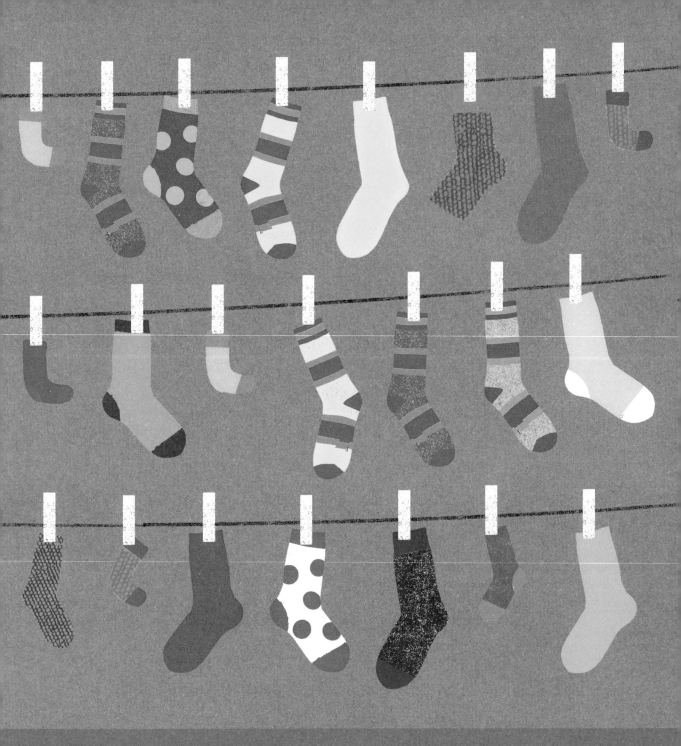

And someone must find
each matching sock pair,
but one is an odd sock
– is it anywhere?

And now there are pairs
of all that you've seen;
pairs of ice creams and planes
and of cats black and lean.

Can you see each pair?
And when you are done,
can you find the thing
of which there's just one?

BIG PICTURE PRESS

www.bigpicturepress.net

First published in the UK in 2016 by Big Picture Press,
part of the Bonnier Publishing Group,
The Plaza, 535 King's Road, London, SW10 0SZ
www.bigpicturepress.net
www.bonnierpublishing.com

ISBN 978-1-78370-463-7

This book was typeset in Brown.
The illustrations were created digitally.

Written and edited by Katie Haworth
Printed in China